Daniel Wood

The American Sharp-Shooter

A Treatise on Gunnery

Daniel Wood

The American Sharp-Shooter
A Treatise on Gunnery

ISBN/EAN: 9783337191672

Printed in Europe, USA, Canada, Australia, Japan

Cover: Foto ©Lupo / pixelio.de

More available books at **www.hansebooks.com**

THE
AMERICAN SHARP-SHOOTER:
A TREATISE ON GUNNERY,

ILLUSTRATING THE

PRACTICAL USE OF THE TELESCOPE AS A SIGHT, AS APPLICABLE TO THE RIFLE, RIFLE BATTERY, ARTILLERY, &c.,

DEMONSTRATING

HOW TO SIGHT A GUN—HOW TO ASCERTAIN THE FALL OF THE BALL FOR ALL DISTANCES—HOW TO GET ELEVATION WITHOUT CHANGE OF SIGHT—HOW TO MEASURE DISTANCES BY THE TELESCOPE,

DEFINING

Certain rules by which to strike the object *every shot*, including other useful information for the instruction of the gunner,

BY DANIEL WOOD.

ROCHESTER:
CURTIS, BUTTS & CO., PRINTERS, BUFFALO STREET.
1862.

DEDICATED

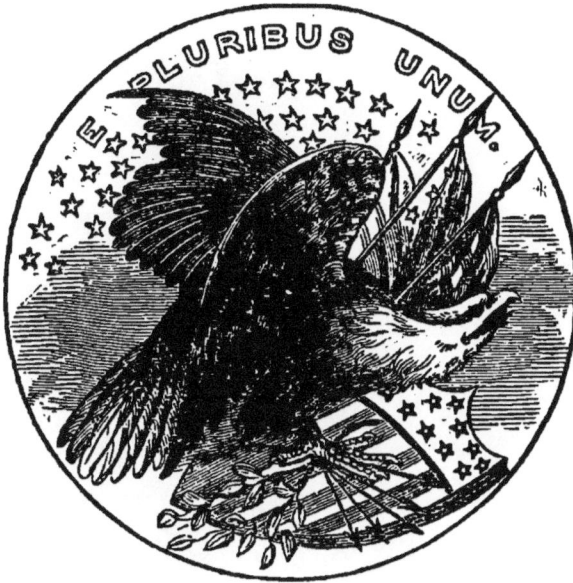

PREFACE.

The time has arrived in our country's history, when every person of suitable age should *at once* acquaint himself with the *use* of military weapons, in order to enable him to act well his part in the great drama of rebellion, which now threatens a dissolution of our sacred and glorious *Union*. A new era in the art of " gunnery " has dawned upon us. The writer, having for some time observed the deficiency that exists in the United States Army in the *practical* and *effective* use of fire-arms, has in the following pages endeavored to impart some *useful information* upon this subject. Every person, whether he be a military man or a civilian, should possess himself of this knowledge at once. To be a "good shot" requires a steady nerve, clear vision, and a correct knowledge of *range, elevation and distance,* and *familiarity with his piece.* A scienced gunner, whether he operates heavy ordnance, artillery, rifle battery, or a rifle, should be able to *strike* his *object every shot.* Even the unerring aim of the skilful " sharp-shooter" would miss "his mark," unless he is fully posted in these rules. How many shots are made without effect to one that hits? In the army a large majority of the soldiers are inexperienced in, and not familiar with, the use of fire-arms, and hence too many random shots are fired, without striking the object intended. It is all important, both in land and naval warfare, that *every shot should tell*. By perusing the sequel, the reader will understand the secret of this success, and thereby acquire a knowledge of the *modus operandi* of accomplishing this much desired result.

ROCHESTER, N. Y., }
November, 1862. }

INTRODUCTION.

In this age of rebellion against the majesty of the American Government, the belligerent spirit of the people is naturally aroused to the subject of self-protection.

A grave attempt is being made to subvert a government republican in form and democratic in principle, which, by a practical experience of over eighty-six years, has proved to be the most perfect, expedient and beneficiary, of any ever instituted on the face of the globe. It guarantees alike all rights of the citizen and of property—encourages and protects all departments of the arts and sciences—of agriculture—and, in fact, all other legitimate pursuits of its subjects, both domestic and foreign.

In such a crisis, the inventive genius of the country is necessarily brought into requisition to discover the most efficient and destructive enginery and implements of warfare, for the purpose of subduing and terminating this most unnatural and unholy resistance to the lawful authority of the government, in the shortest practicable period.

And inasmuch as our unscrupulous enemies have resorted to the force of arms, the arbitrament of military power, to carry out their nefarious project, the people of the loyal States by the pressure of circumstances are compelled, as the last alternative, to resort to the same extreme means of warfare, in self-defence, as well as to reassert the power of the Federal Government over all its extended dominions.

The suppression of this arrogant rebellion must and shall be accomplished, and all the legitimate prerogatives of the Federal Government should be speedily and powerfully exerted for that purpose, and such a lesson taught to all traitors, that a like experiment will never again be attempted.

The object of these articles is more particularly directed to one branch of the military service of the country—to illustrate the practical and effective use of fire arms—such as artillery, rifle batteries, &c., having reference more particularly to the Telescopic Rifle, and especially to the use of the Telescope, as a *sight, in measuring distances and ascertaining elevations.*

The subject of "gunnery" and of "projectiles," has, of course, engaged the attention of the scientific military men of all ages and countries, but there are many points of very great importance, although simple, which, to the knowledge of the writer, have not been fully or clearly developed, or put into *practical use.*

Our aim is to present a few useful lessons and rules for the benefit and guidance of the "gunner," whether he operates a " telescopic rifle," rifle battery, cannon, or guns of larger calibre, and whether at short or long range.

Among the qualifications of a skilful, accurate and effective " gunner," we would name the following :

1st. A keen eye, quick perception, and steady nerve.

2d. A good judge of distances, both horizontal, perpendicular, and longitudinal.

3d. A correct idea of the size of objects by comparison or otherwise, both longitudinal, latitudinal, and altitudinal ; a practical knowledge of the use and objects of the Telescope and Telescopic Sight, in measuring distances, &c.

5th. How to sight a gun readily and accurately.

6th. An *actual experimental* knowledge of the fall of the ball for all distances.

The rapid fall of the ball in gunnery at different distances, and especially at long ranges, is a great impediment to be overcome, and it requires much judgment, calculation, and experiment. We now allude to perpendicular range. So also the effect of the atmosphere, wind, &c., on the ball while in motion, which we call horizontal range, requires practice, skill, and care, to calculate correctly.

Hence no gunner can strike an object without first knowing the *distance*, and the *elevation required*, and a proper calculation for the effects of the atmosphere on the projectile.

No person can be said to be a good gunner, or should go into the army, especially with a Telescopic Rifle, without first ascertaining by actual experiment, the fall of his ball for every point of distance, from the shortest to the longest range. For instance, at 10, 40, 80, 100, 160, rods, up to any required distance. The result of these experiments should be noted down, or committed to memory, so that no errors should occur.

For target shooting you should ascertain the fall of the ball for every five rods.

Having settled this, the next and *equally important thing* to be ascertained is the *distance*, in order to get a *correct elevation*.

This will be explained in a subsequent article. (Article 4.)

We propose to illustrate our subject in the following articles, having reference to the use of the ordinary Telescopic Sight, which shows the object in its natural position, and not inverted.

Article 1.—The Telescopic Sight. Its use and superior advantages.

Article 2.—How to Sight a gun. Calculations for the wind. How to ascertain the fall of the ball for different distances. Target practice, &c.

ARTICLE 3.—Importance of numerous cross-hairs. How to get elevation without changing the sight, and without either raising or lowering the Telescope.

ARTICLE 4.—How to measure or calculate distances by means of the Telescope.

ARTICLE 5.—Practical observations. General use of the Telescope as a distance glass, as applicable to Artillery, Rifle Batteries, &c.

In our observations upon these topics it is not our intention to present a labored treatise on the science of "gunnery" in general, which would require too much time and space fully to develop, a work which we may at some future period undertake, should occasion and circumstances warrant. But for the present, we shall content ourselves with such lessons, rules and suggestions in the premises as occur to us to be of *immense practical use and importance* to every person, whether he be a *soldier, officer* or *private*, or a civilian. It is suggested that at all times, whether in *peace* or *war*, it is the duty of every citizen to study and familiarize himself with the use of fire arms, not only for self defence, but to be ready for any and every emergency that might arise. But especially *in time of war* every man in the public service, whether officer or private, should at once be thoroughly posted in the art of gunnery, so that *every shot will tell. That he shoots to kill.*

No soldier can be said to be a perfect gunner, or should claim the appellation of " sharp-shooter," unless he can hit his mark *the first shot*, whatever the distance may be, within the random or range of his gun. Every army officer should understand and become familiar with this subject, and every private should be drilled in this respect as much as in any other branch of military tactics.

Every soldier knows how to load and fire a gun. Is this all he is required to know? Of *all the shots fired, does one in a thousand hit the object aimed at?*

With these introductory remarks we will now proceed to point out to you certain rules and regulations by which this can be done with approximate certainty *every shot.*

ARTICLE 1.

The Telescopic Sight—Its Use and Advantages.

Among the practical benefits gained by the use of the Telescope are, that the objects to be seen are more clearly presented to the view by the magnifying power of the lenses used. Its superiority, like other optical instruments, is most apparent at long ranges when the object cannot be distinctly discernable by the naked eye. No sight ever invented in gunnery affords more pleasure, satisfaction and accuracy, either for hunting game, target practice, or "rebel shooting," than the "Telescopic." The more it is used and understood, the more it will be appreciated and come into general practice.

Experience will demonstrate that more care and perfection is necessary in the construction of these instruments, and of the manner of their attachment to the gun. They should be so firmly and securely fastened that no errors or variations arise from this cause.

The common mode of lowering or elevating this sight for different distances has been by means of a thumb-screw near the eye glass, intended to be exactly perpendicular, to be turned up or down, as occasion may require. Another mode is, that instead of the screw, a piston, or straight rod of iron or steel, is used to move up and down in a perpendicular line, held or adjusted by a small thumb-screw at the side.

But in all these modes of fastenings there are more or less errors and variations, so that perfect accuracy cannot be attained. It is almost impossible to make this screw or piston rod exactly plumb, and if it is not, the turning up or down will cause a deviation of the telescope to the right or left of perpendicular, and hence the line of vision through the glass would be varied accordingly.

To avoid these errors and irregularities, as well as the time and trouble necessary to turn up or down for every designated distance, the writer has substituted a new method of elevation, without the "turning or raising up" process, which will be explained in Article 3.

We would recommend another improvement which is of much practical benefit and advantage. The tube of the telescope should not extend to, nor within five or six inches of, the muzzle of the gun. In this way you can handle the gun at the muzzle more easily, attended with greater convenience in the process of loading and wiping out, and besides you will not be so likely to hazard the breaking of the object glass of your telescope, as you otherwise would, nor would the smoke from the discharge of the gun be so apt to obscure the glass.

As to the length or size of the Telescope, much

would depend upon the particular use intended. For long distances, and, indeed, for the purposes of elevation, a large field of vision is desirable. The objects would appear more clear and distinct. The ordinary diameter of the tube is from four to seven-eighths of an inch. We would recommend for army guns a Telescopic tube of about one inch in diameter to the exterior circumference, leaving about seven-eighths of an inch for the diameter of the internal circumference, as guns of this description are generally of heavier calibre than the common rifle.

In the ordinary Telescope but two hairs are used, attached to a circle or frame inserted in the tube of the telescope at the focal distance of the eye glass, crossing each other at right angles, one perpendicular and the other horizontal, as illustrated by the following diagram, which is intended to be about seven-eighths of an inch in diameter.

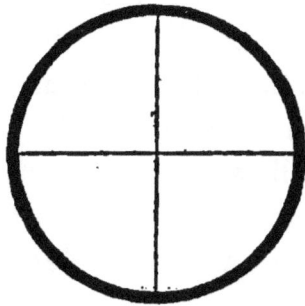

In sighting, the point at which these hairs cross each other, is to be placed upon the centre of the object aimed at, and in all cases great care and caution should be exercised in holding the piece firm and steady, and in obtaining a clear and perfect vision, and for this purpose the eye should be placed as near as practicable to the eye-glass.

It should be observed that these cross hairs should be very fine; the finer the better, (as they are enlarged in proportion to the magnifying power of the glasses used,) so that they will tend less to obstruct the vision, or to conceal the object aimed at, and will enable the gunner to draw a closer sight.

But in the military service the telescope becomes still more useful, and is indispensable. The magnifying or microscopic power of the instrument depends upon the distance at which the objects are viewed. Their importance is illustrated in viewing the enemy's works, such as forts, arsenals, fortifications, breast-works, position and movement of their men and guns, their war vessels and armament, and how manned, in examining at a distance the surface of the country, the kind and number of the enemy's forces, such as militia, cavalry, artillery batteries, &c., and to distinguish officers from privates.

Thus it will be seen that the telescope becomes an important optical instrument, not only as a *sight*, *but as a field or distance glass.*

Its usefulness is not confined to the rifle and the *sharp shooter*, but may be applied with equal force to the rifle battery, artillery, and the gunner generally.

Its superior advantages will more clearly appear in the succeeding articles.

ARTICLE 2.

How to Sight a gun—Calculations for the wind—How to ascertain the fall of the ball for different distances—Target Practice, &c.

How to Sight a gun—Calculations for the wind, &c.

To this first proposition no explanation seems to be required. Its solution appears so simple that one would say at once, that any person who ever shot a gun, ought to know how to do this. So he does, in the old fashioned way, by a long process of trial shots. But how many shots would it require, and how long would it take him? Suppose the first shot you make should hit a foot over or two feet under the centre of the target, how much would you have to turn up or down to strike the centre? Have you any rule for your guide, or can you ascertain otherwise than by repeated experimental shots until you strike the centre? This is all random work; you may do it in five, or it might require ten shots.

Now, the writer proposes to give you a certain rule by which you can do it the *second shot.* We say second shot, because it is necessary in all cases to make one shot first in order to ascertain where your rifle carries. Knowing this, you can, the second shot, strike the centre of the target, or a line horizontal with it.

We are now speaking of sighting the gun for perpendicular range—that is, up and down—and not horizontal, or right and left.

ILLUSTRATION.

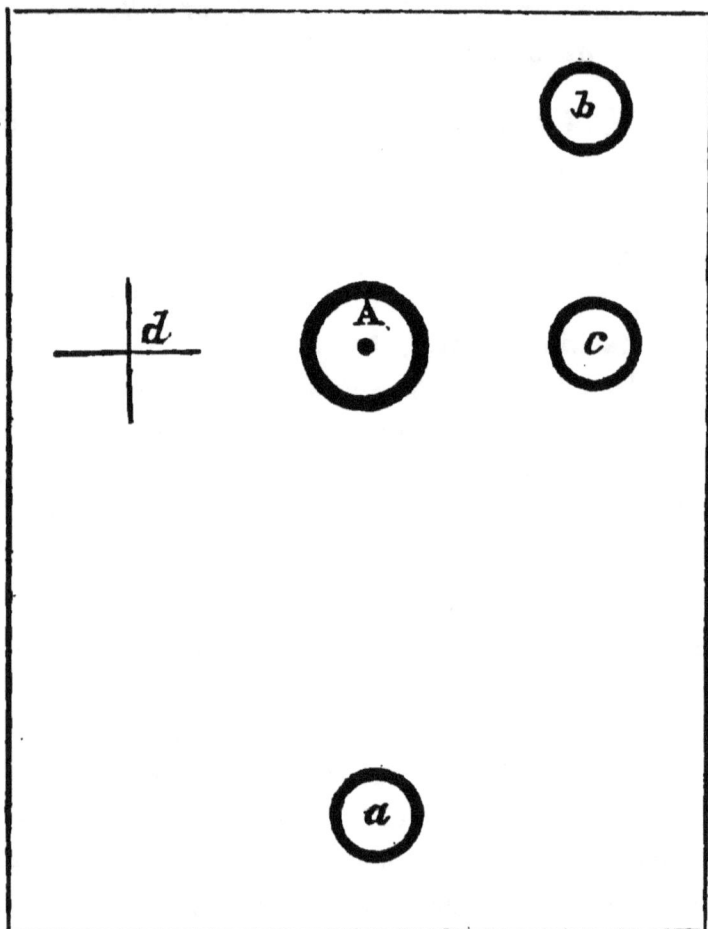

In this diagram *A* represents the target, which you wish to hit. Suppose you aim at the centre of the target and your first ball strikes at (*a*,) say a foot in a direct line under. After this shot you will then look through your telescope at the target, and you will see the target and the ball hole of the first shot. But if the distance is so great that the magnifying power of your glasses does not enable you to see the ball hole distinctly, that, then some object easily discernible, such as a red wafer, or other colored substance of suitable size, should be placed over the ball hole. You will then sight on the centre of the target, and hold the gun firm and immovable while you turn up until the cross-hairs centre the ball hole (*a*) below. By this process of elevation you perceive you have raised the ball up just as much as it fell under before, or in other words you have brought your line of sight and ball hole together, (a point at which the line of sight and tragectile meet, and which is called the *point blank* range,) and your next shot sighted on the target must strike the centre, providing there is no error in your calculations and your vision accurate.

Again, suppose your first shot strikes at letter (*b*,) six inches above and to the right of the centre of the target, you will then, as before, sight on the target, and hold the gun firm and stationary while you turn down until the cross-hairs centre the upper ball hole, and your next shot sighted on the target will of course strike at (*c*,) on a horizontal line with the centre of the target, on account of the horizontal range not being correct.

By this simple process you have acquired your perpendicular range, as you see, in two shots, and with *perfect accuracy*

The next step is to get your horizontal range. This you must do by moving your sight either to the right or left, as occasion may require; or you can make a calculation by the glass by aiming the same distance to the right or left, as the case may be.

For instance, suppose your ball strikes at (*a,*) which is three inches to the right of the target, you can aim three inches to the left, at (*d,*) and you will strike the centre, the same as though you had changed your sight accordingly.

As a general rule, in respect to horizontal range, the safest way is to sight your gun in a still, clear day, when there is no wind to vary the ball, and then continue the same permanently, or have your sight marked when correctly adjusted, and not change it for the purpose of attempting to counteract the effects of the wind. The wind is a very uncertain element to contend with. At one moment it is furious, at another moderate, and then a calm; so that to keep apace with its fluctuations you would be compelled, in this way, to keep changing your sight continually, and then you would gain but an approximate accuracy.

On the other hand, by the mode first suggested you can with more ease and certainty accomplish the same result, for by the glass you can always, on short range, see your last shot, and from that you can readily calculate for the next, better and more correctly, than by the delay and trouble of changing your sight to meet the momentary shifting of the wind.

To illustrate, suppose the wind varies the ball six inches to the right, now, as you can see the ball hole and the target, you can easily, if the wind is the same, aim six inches to the left, and then you would strike the target the next shot.

We venture to say that you cannot in one chance in ten, so change your sight at one experiment as to accomplish the same result. In case you succeed, when the wind has subsided you must change back again, and then you may not adjust it exactly as it was when you began.

So it will readily be perceived, that this perpetual alteration of sights for any purpose will continually involve you in uncertainty, and is of doubtful practice.

We will now turn our attention to the proposition:

How to ascertain the fall of the ball for different distances—Target practice, &c.

To illustrate this we propose the following target:

10 rods.	A	
20 rods.	a	3 in.
25 rods.	b	6 in.
30 rods.	c	12 in.
35 rods.	d	18 in.
40 rods.	e	80 in.

It must be borne in mind that in these experiments the gunner must use the same gun, sight, charge of powder, ball and patch.

In the first place you must sight your gun accurately at the target, *A*, at short distance, say ten rods. You will then put your target off at twenty rods, and fire at same target with same sight as before, and the result will be your ball will strike at (*a*,) or about three inches below. Then at 25 rods, and so on for any required distance, and the result will be about as above indicated up to 40 rods, depending, of course, upon the calibre of the gun, weight and size of ball, and charge of powder used, viz:

At 20 rods the ball falls about					3 inches.
" 25	"	"	-	- 6	"
" 30	"	"	-	12	"
" 35	"	"	-	- 18	"
" 40	"	"	-	- 30	"
" 50	"	"	-	- 4 ft. 8	"
" 60	"	"	-	7 ft. 8	"
" 70	"	"	-	- 12 ft.	
" 80	"	∕ "	-	18 ft.	

The implements used in these trials was a rifle, with a barrel weighing eight pounds and 29 inches in length, with a conical ball weighing 65 to the pound, and Hazard's No. 1 F powder, with 2¼ inches of bore of the gun to the charge, and at rest, with telescopic sight.

In target practice the best form of target the writer has discovered is a paste-board with white surface, with a red centre, such as a red wafer, size from 1 to 3 inches, depending upon the distance, clearness of atmosphere and distinctness of vision. The pasteboard is preferred for its adhesive properties, because the ball, in perforating it, does not tear the surface, but makes a hole just the size of the ball, and the same can more readily be seen by the glass. The red or wafer centre is selected because while it can be clearly seen, in case a ball penetrates it, it can be more readily discovered through the glass than any other color, and thereby avoids the necessity of examining the target at each shot.

In order to make a close, even string, many nice points are to be observed :

1st. The target should be placed as near as practicable in range of the wind, (if any,) and not crossways, if you desire to avoid as far as possible the effect of the wind upon the ball. You should also shoot in a direction from the sun, as by this course the target and ball holes can be more readly seen, and, besides, the reflection of the sun will not dazzle or obscure your vision through the telescope.

2d. Great firmness and steadiness in holding the gun, (which should always be held in the same position, plumb, determinable by range through either your horizontal or perpendicular hair,) and a clear sight, are required.

3d. The gun should be wiped out each shot.

4th. The weight and kind of ball, and charge of powder and patch, should be the same each shot.

5th. In case there is any wind, particular care should be exercised in making calculations for the horizontal variation of the ball.

In order to carry out these suggestions to a practical and satisfactory result, extreme vigilance and caution is necessary, and your gun in all its parts, with all its fixtures and appendages, should be as perfect as modern improvements would indicate.

In target practice ten consecutive shots are usually called " a string." The result is ascertained in this way: Measure from the centre of the target to the centre of each ball hole or shot, and the aggregate of the whole ten shots will be the measurement of the string. And the same rule of measurement applies to a string of any greater or less number of shots.

To make a good string the greatest precision is necessary. Beware of wild shots, for one roving shot may count more than the whole remaining nine, and lose you the string. Close and even shooting is the best evidence of a good marksman.

But in case your telescope is attached so as to be moved horizontally by a thumb-screw, then you can get your horizontal range by observing the target and ball hole, in the same manner as above described for perpendicular range.

*Importance of numerous cross-hairs—How to get ele
vation without changing the sight, and without either raising or lowering the telescope.*

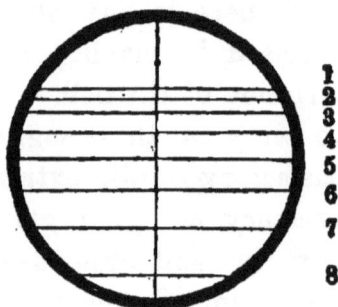

By reference to the above diagram it will be seen
that eight horizontal cross-hairs parallel to each other
at different distances, are inserted. These hairs, as
before mentioned, are attached to a frame located
within the tube of the telescope, next in front, and
at the focal distance of, the eye glass. The number
to be used may be more or less, as experience may
dictate to be of the most practical benefit.

For the purposes of illustration we shall call them
"distance hairs," numbering from the top down, 1,
2, 3, &c. These hairs are intended to represent the
fall of the ball at different distances, and should be

so arranged as to be in exact ratio with and to correspond to it. For instance:

No. 1 is intended for short range, say - 10 rods.
"   2   "   "   "   - - 20 "
"   3   "   "   "   30 "
"   4   "   "   "   - - 40 "
"   5   "   "   "   -   50 "
"   6   "   "   "   - - 60 "
"   7   "   "   "   -   70 "
"   8   "   "   "   - - 80 "

The numbers, as you see, correspond with the figures representing the distances, so as to be the more readily remembered. You will, of course, first sight your gun accurately for the short distance, say ten rods, by the upper cross-hair, No. 1. This done, your gun will then be sighted for all distances indicated by the several cross-hairs: No. 2 for 20 rods, No. 3 for 30 rods, &c., up to 80 rods, without any alteration or elevation of your telescope.

By this means of elevation you avoid the errors consequent upon the turning up process. I have only intended to illustrate the principle, and the arrangement of the cross-hairs, as above indicated, is for short ranges. In case you desired to shoot at longer ranges, you can do it in three ways.

1st. By arranging your cross-hairs farther apart.

2d. By turning up for any distance beyond eighty rods.

3d. By using the cross-hairs as arranged above, in this manner: Sight your gun by the upper hair at 40 rods instead of 10, and then your elevation will be for different distances, about as follows : 2d hair, 50 rods; 3d hair, 60 rods; 4th hair, 70 rods; 5th hair, 80 rods ; 6th hair, 90 rods; 7th hair, 100 rods; 8th hair, 110 rods. Or you may have to alternate or skip a hair at extreme distances. Or you can sight your upper hair at 80 rods, and the same ratio of elevation for different distances beyond that will follow, as graduated by the separate distance hairs below.

This process ot elevation is simple and yet accurate. All that is required is to *become familiar with it by practice.* This knowledge once acquired, you will have no difficulty in ascertaining your elevation at once, and with unerring accuracy. This, of course, has reference solely to perpendicular range. You must calculate for a variation of the ball by the wind, &c., in respect to horizontal range, as hereinbefore mentioned.

It will be observed that these hairs are not equidistant from each other. The reason is obvious. The path of the ball in motion as it is discharged from the gun forms the line of a parabola; the farther the ball is projected, the more rapid it inclines downward by the force of gravitation, and in an inverse ratio to the distance it travels, until it strikes some object or its force is spent.

As these hairs are intended to represent the fall of the ball at different distances, and as the ball falls faster the farther it goes, the lower hairs answering the longer ranges, must, consequently, be farther apart, as illustrated in the diagram heading this article.

In order to ascertain the correct location of these horizontal distance hairs, and the space that should separate them from each other, the following test may be resorted to:

Take for illustration the target referred to in Article 2, (page 24.) Sight your upper cross-hair (No. 1) on the centre of this target, and, holding it there at rest, you will then examine through your telescope the separate ball holes of your shots at the different distances, and see if the several corresponding distance hairs cover the ball holes represented by them. If they do, then they are correct. If not, you will note what variation is required, so that they can be adjusted accordingly.

But suppose these cross-hairs are not arranged in exact accordance with the several distances they are intended respectively to represent. We will point out another interesting rule to guide you in sighting, upon which it will be well to practice in order to familiarize yourself with the use of the telescope, so that you can acquire the *art of getting sight and range with celerity.*

Assume, now, that you put up a mark at any imaginable distance, and fire at the centre, sighting through the upper hair. You will then observe the ball hole, and ascertain the cross-hair on or nearest to it, and at the next shot you will sight on the target through the cross-hair which appeared to be at or in nearest proximity to the ball hole of the first shot. In case neither cross-hair comes in exact range with the ball hole of the prior shot, you can sight by the cross-hair nearest to it on the mark, making your calculations for what variation there may be, whether above or below. This will subserve all practical purposes, such as shooting game, or large objects, except, perhaps, you desire to make a close and even target string.

As alluded to in our introductory remarks, the above arrangement of the cross or distance hairs, has reference to a telescope which reflects the objects in their natural position, and not inverted. Should a telescope be used which inverts the objects, the arrangement of the distance-hairs, instead of the above form, should be reversed or inverted. For example, No. 1 should be at the bottom, running up to No. 8 at the top. In the latter case, you sight through your lower hair (No. 1) for the short distance, 10 rods, and No. 2 for 20 rods, and so on up to 80 rods.

ARTICLE 4.

*How to measure or calculate distances by means of the
telescope.*

To illustrate this proposition we shall have occasion to refer again to the following diagram :

We assume the cross-hairs to be arranged in this form, as they can be used for a two-fold purpose, viz: The first for a ten rod sight and the second for twenty rods, and the two together as a means of measuring or ascertaining distances.

Let us now call your attention to cross-hairs Nos. 1 and 2. On looking through your telescope at an object or a target at 10 rods distant you will observe the space intervening between the delineation these two hairs make as they strike the object. You will find it will be 1½ inches. Then put your object off 20 rods, and you will find the space, on looking thro' your glass, to be 3 inches ; and for other distances up to one mile, as designated in the following

2

TABLE.

Showing the space between these cross-hairs as they strike the object as it appears through the telescope, for every ten rods up to 320 rods, or one mile, viz:

Spaces.		Distances.
$1\frac{1}{2}$ inches,	....	10 rods.
3 "	....	20 "
$4\frac{1}{2}$ "	....	30 "
6 "	....	40 "
$7\frac{1}{2}$ "	....	50 "
9 "	....	60 "
$10\frac{1}{2}$ "	....	70 "
12 "	....	80 "
$13\frac{1}{2}$ "	....	90 "
15 "	....	100 "
$16\frac{1}{2}$ "	....	110 "
18 "	....	120 "
$19\frac{1}{2}$ "	....	130 "
21 "	....	140 "
$22\frac{1}{2}$ "	....	150 "
24 "	....	160 "
$25\frac{1}{2}$ "	....	170 "
27 "	....	180 "
$28\frac{1}{2}$ "	....	190 "
30 "	....	200 "
$31\frac{1}{2}$ "	....	210 "
33 "	....	220 "
$34\frac{1}{2}$ "	....	230 "

Spaces.	Distances.
36 inches,	....240 rods.
37½ "	....250 "
39 "	................260 "
40½ "	................270 "
42 "	.. ..280 "
43½ "	. ... 290 "
45 "	................300 "
46½ "	.... 310 "
48 "	................320 "

and the same exact ratio or proportion for any desired distance within the optical range of your telescope.

From this it will be seen that the apparent open-
ing or space between these hairs in their demarka-
tion upon the object is extended just 1¼ inches for
every ten rods of elongated distance.

Observe, also, as an optical and geometrical truth,
that whatever distance these hairs are apart, as they
appear on the object, at say ten rods, whether 1, 2,
or 3 inches, depending upon the proximity of the
hairs to each other, they will exhibit the same proportion at any other distance at which the object can
be seen, as the range of vision through these hairs
diverge in straight lines forming an angle at the eye.
Any person can test the correctness of this by his own
telescope, arranged as herein indicated, with a very
little observation and practice.

Having first ascertained the optical range of these two hairs, as here proposed, accurately for different distances, and determined the exact spaces between them as they appear on the object every separate and distinct distance, the next question to be solved is, how is this to be applied in measuring or determining the horizontal space between you and the object in view.

This proposition we will now proceed to demonstrate. In the first place you should, by measurement and comparison, practically familiarize yourself with the size of different objects, as, for instance, the size of the head or body of a man, horse, ox, cow, dog, cat, or other animals; the height or diameter of a wagon wheel, height of a fence, door, or window of a house, or any other object which you can readily see or discover through your glass. The size of such familiar objects you can readily calculate, or perhaps may know with approximate exactness.

Having fixed in your mind the size or altitude of these different objects, you can readily apply the rule of measurement above indicated by the cross-hairs in your glass, to the distance between you and the object sought. To illustrate, suppose in your surveys at a distance you observe an object and desire to ascertain how far it is off. Take for instance, a man; you will see his head or face, which is about say 9 inches in length, perpendicular. You will then examine the object through your glass, at rest, by ranging hair No. 1 at the upper edge or side of the head, and ascertain where hair No. 2 strikes. If at the chin or lower part, your hairs separate just 9 inches. Hence, according to the rule, and by reference to the table above mentioned, the object is 60 rods distant, for at this distance, the lines of these two hairs separate on striking the object exactly 9 inches.

Again, suppose these two cross-hairs covers but one half of the size of the man's head, which is 4½ inches, then, of course, your object is 30 rods off. Or in case the hairs should separate twice the length of the head, which you can easily judge, then, as a consequence, the hairs separate 18 inches, and the distance would be 120 rods.

Take, also, the head of a horse as a representation. You will find on examination that all horses' heads average about the same length, and will not vary an inch from two feet in vertical size. By applying the rule as last suggested to this case, the following will be the result: If the cross-hairs just take in the head, which is 24 inches, the animal is exactly 160 rods, or half a mile off. So, again, if the cross-hairs covers one half of the size of the head, which is 12 inches, the object is 80 rods, or a quarter of a mile distant. Or in case the separation of the hairs should appear twice the length of the head, or 48 inches, the object would be 320 rods off, or just one mile. The same rule is equally applicable to longer dis-

tances, as 1, 2, 3, 4, or 5 miles, or any required distance within the random or range of your piece, and
at which the objects can be clearly and distinctly
seen through the glass.

Imagine yourself at a fort on the beach of the
ocean, and you discover an enemy's vessel or "man
of war" at a distance at sea, and your sole object is
to strike her the *first shot*. Knowing the elevation
of your cannon for each interval of space within its
range, the *next and all important fact*, to be determined, is, the *distance*. You will then, through your
glass, examine some object on board of the ship, the
size or altitude of which is familiar to you, such, for
instance, as a man, it may be a sailor or soldier, a
horse, sail, mast, smoke-pipe, or other thing observa-
ble on board. Take the man, for instance, who is
about six feet in height, and you will discover, in
case the line of the cross-hairs range one at the top
of his head and the other at his feet, that the hairs
separate just six feet, and the distance is 480 rods, or
1½ miles. Should the hairs show twice the height of
the man, or 12 feet, the distance would be 960 rods,
or 3 miles. So also in case they show but one half
of the man's altitude, 3 feet, the distance would be
240 rods. The result would be, you would strike
this ship *every shot*, if within the reach of your gun,
and you get the corresponding elevation.

From these illustrations the application of the rules
and principles herein inculcated, appears at once easy

and simple, and with proper *drill and practice* in this respect, great certainty, precision and accuracy may be attained.

It should be observed, as before intimated, that for long distances the lenses in the telescope should be more powerful, and the diameter of the tube about one inch, in order to afford a larger field of vision, and the cross-hairs should be black, so that the lines of them can be more distinctly traced on the object, and as fine as possible, so that the enlargement of them by the magnifying power of the glass will obscure the object as little as practicable. Besides, the more delicate the hairs, the more accurate and minute will be the measurement of distant objects.

Again, in cases where it is not convenient or practicable to attach the telescope to the piece as a sight, it may be used as a field glass, or as an optical *locometer*, (a measurer of space or distance by the glass,) separately, with equal advantage. If used for *this purpose only,* but two parallel cross-hairs would be necessary.

As a matter of convenience, it would be well to so arrange the cross-hairs, that the spaces between them should be one inch as they separate on the object at 10 rods distant. It would at 20 rods be 2 inches, at 30 rods, 3 inches, and so on at the same ratio for every 10 rods. By this arrangement the luminous space between the lines of the hairs would be increased one inch for every ten rods, and as seen above, the numeral figures representing the space between the hairs *in inches*, corresponds with that of the distance it measures *in rods*. This assimilation of figures would enable you the more readily to remember the perpendicular mensuration of the space between the horizontal parallel hairs, which correspond to and represent, the space or distance they measure horizontally, viz., 1 inch, 10 rods: 2 inches, 20 rods: 3 inches, 30 rods: 4 inches, 40 rods, &c. In other words, to render it more simple, multiply the distance between the hairs *in inches* by 10, and the product will be the distance measured *in rods*.

It should also be remarked, what, doubtless, has already occurred to the reader, that by the arrangement of the cross-hairs in this close proximity to each other, he will be enabled to make a more accurate and exact measurement of the height of distant objects through the glass than otherwise, much, of course, depending upon the fine and subtle texture of the cross-lines.

We deem the matters treated of in this article of so much moment, that we would recommend to every gunner the importance of continued and unremitted practice until he familiarizes himself with the rules and regulations herein prescribed, and their application to the subject, and their fitness for the objects and purposes designed.

ARTICLE 5.

*Practical observations—General use of the Telescope
as a distance glass—As applicable to
Artillery, Rifle Batteries, &c.*

From the sentiments already expressed upon the
various subjects indicated, many useful and important lessons may be derived. There is, perhaps, no
principle in the science of gunnery which is so *little
understood or practiced* as the art of acquiring accurate *elevation, range,* and *distance.* Without a thor-
ough knowledge of these pre-requisites no person
can be said to be a *good gunner,* an *effective artiller-
ist,* or an *expert sharp-shooter.*

In all the various departments of military operations there is no branch of the public service, which
contributes to advantage and victory so much as the
efficient use of ordnance and fire-arms. The most
important feature in gunnery to insure success is, to
know the distance to the object which you wish to strike.
In the absence of this, all must be the result of mere
conjecture or accident. All other elements may be
more readily understood or easily acquired.

We claim to have solved this one great mystery,
and to have overcome what heretofore seemed to be
ar insurmountable difficulty. If we have succeeded,
one cf the prominent objects of our task will have

been accomplished. But the field of our observations, for practical purposes, should not be thus circumscribed. We hold it to be the imperative duty of every *citizen* and *patriot*, to contribute both his mental and physical energies to aid his country in this, her hour of peril, to sustain the *integrity* of the American *Union*—to subjugate those in rebellion, and to mete out to all traitors their merited doom. In a word, the whole power of the general government should be exerted for the accomplishment of this object. We are digressing, but a sense of true patriotism is our only apology.

In the foregoing pages we have treated the telescope principally as a sight for rifle shooting, measuring distances, &c. Its capacity for usefulness in the army is not among the least of its claims to superiority. The natural vision is short, confined and obscure, and needs some artificial auxiliary to extend its optical power to more distant objects. The telescope, or field glass, is intended to supply this defect. It is valuable not only as a field glass, but as a *locometer*, when arranged for that purpose, and in the manner hereinbefore described.

The observations we have made touching the use of the telescope as a sight to a rifle for the sharpshooter, and in enabling him *to sight his gun to get elevation*, and to *measure distances*, apply with equal force to the effective working of *artillery* and the *rifle battery*. Why not attach it as a sight to the centre barrel of the rifle battery ? By this means the gunner could more readily and clearly see dis-tant objects, *measure his distance* with more accuracy, get his elevation more easily, and his shots would thereby be far more effective. And even so with ar-tillery. But if this is impracticable, then certainly its use would be equally apparent as a field glass and a *locometer.*

For example, suppose you observe at a distance a body of Rebel infantry or cavalry, and you wish to fire your artillery among them with certain effect. Knowing your *elevation for all distances*, the first fact to be ascertained is the *distance* intervening between you and the object. Having one of these instruments in your hand, you will, at once, by observation through it, examine the apparent objects before you, selecting out such an one, as a man, horse, &c., the size or height of which you know, and which just fills the open space between your cross-hairs, and in case it is a man six feet high, the distance would be just 1¼ miles. Therefore by elevating your piece to the 1¼ mile range, your shot would certainly not be with-out effect.

So, this would be equally true in case your mark was the enemy's war-vessel, gun boat, fort, fortifica-tions, or other public works.

So *with the rifle battery.* How *important* and ne-cessary then is it that you know your *elevation and distance*, if you would strike your object the *first*, as well as *every successive shot.* In this instance, it would seem to be the more indispensable, for if you miss your object one shot, the whole twenty-five cotemporaneous shots are lost; whereas, on the contrary, the whole would take effect, and hence this battery would be a most *destructive engine of warfare.* Inasmuch as, with a proper knowledge of *elevation* and *distance,* this piece would throw *twenty-five effective* shots at *every discharge,* which are made in quick succession, at the rate of from 8 to 12 per minute.

We have thus far adverted to the telescope as an instrument of great power and usefulness, as connected with a subject of greater magnitude, viz., the army and navy.

To the *sportsman* this instrument is also important and interesting, but, perhaps, in a less commensurate degree. Before the unerring aim of the hunter, peering through the bright and clear vision of his telescope, his game, however small, will scarcely hope to escape the fatal shot.

The rules we have defined as to the uses and purposes to which this instrument can be applied, may be appropriated for the benefit of the every day man in his out-door sports. It may be, you are roaming through the fields and forests on a hunting expedition, and your eye catches at a distance a crow or a hawk. You are ruminating in your mind, "if I miss this bird the first shot, he is off. How can I engineer to hit him? I know my elevation, now if I could only know the distance, I'm all right. How can I ascertain this? Must I guess at it, and let it go at that?"

Our response to this last interrogation is, no. Let us see if we can enlighten you on this subject. The vertical size of the bird is say 6 inches. I look at it and apply my rule of measurement by the cross-hairs, and find that their space of separation just covers his body, and hence he is exactly 40 rods distant. I fire at him, ranging through my 4th hair, (being my 40 rod elevation,) and down comes the game, doomed to certain death. And so of any other game or object where the *distance is unknown*.

The more enlarged views a person has upon this subject, the more important and useful does it appear. The more reflection the writer has given, the more is impressed upon his mind, the *necessity* of *drilling every officer and private* in the army in the theory and art of gunnery, with respect to getting *range, acquiring elevation,* and *ascertaining distances,* under the guidance of the *rules and principles herein promulgated,* as much or more than in any other branch of military tactics. For, certainly, without this, all would be error, chance, uncertainty.

All shooting or firing of projectiles must of necessity be experimental and without effect, except by accident, where the *distance is unknown.* On the contrary, knowing this all-important fact, or *having in your possession the means of ascertaining it at once,* you are fully *armed* and *equipped,* ready for any and every emergency, and amply prepared to shoot down your traitorous foe with unerring certainty.

By a *practical knowledge* of the truths here revealed universally disseminated throughout the whole army, all *chance and fortuitous shots* would be avoided, and thereby much time, labor, and ammunition, would be saved, which would furnish an item of no small magnitude in economy to the government.

To *our friend*, the *sharp-shooter, with his telescopic rifle,* we desire to impart a little familiar, friendly, parting advice. You are about (if you have not a'ready done so,) to embark in a new enterprise ; to explore a new field of operations ; to seek what the wild Indian would most desire, *a new hunting ground.* You have entered the United States army in defence of your country in this, the darkest era in her history. For this *volunteering* act of patriotism, your children, and your chidren's children, will rise up and call you blessed. Future history will record your name as one of the *sharp-shooter's* on the side of the *Union* in the great *Southern rebellion* of 1861. Let us exhort you in language analagous to that of revolutionary times : "I know not what course others may take, but as for me, give *me liberty* or give me *death.*" "Live or die, sink or swim, survive or perish, I am for" the *American Union.*

But to the subject. You are just entering the arena of *rebel hunting* and *traitor shooting.* A novel kind of *gaming* for this *age* and *country.* But having enlisted in this cause, it becomes you to exert all the means in your power, not only for self-preservation, but also for the immediate suppression of this infamous rebellion. For this purpose always be vigilant, that your rifle, telescope and other implements belonging therewith, are as perfect as possible and in order. Familiarize yourself, *by practice*, with your gun and telescope, in respect *to fall of ball, elevation* and *distance*. Should you be an officer, see to it, that every private in your company is thoroughly drilled in the use of the rifle, and especially of this instrument. For with a perfect knowledge of these, success will attend you, and your shots will be certain and effective.

Whatever may be the object aimed at, whether it be a *rebel gunner* or *officer* whom you wish to pick off, with proper coolness and care, observing the rules of elevation and of *ascertaining the distance*, you *cannot fail* to *discharge* the *fatal shot*. By this means you will have successfully accomplished the great end of your mission.

In conclusion permit us to say that we have endeavored thus briefly to present our subject in a manner so plain, and with illustrations so simple, that any person of ordinary understanding can readily comprehend it. We have aimed to be entirely practical.

If we have succeeded in affording any new light or knowledge in the art and theory of gunnery, or any important information upon the *practical* and *effective use of* fire-arms, or in enlisting more interest in, or inaugurating a new impulse in relation thereto, we shall be content, and our labor not in vain.

We therefore submit our work in this crude form to the candid judgment and patronage of the public.

www.ingramcontent.com/pod-product-compliance
Lightning Source LLC
Chambersburg PA
CBHW032134080426
42733CB00008B/1067